CROSSING THE LADDER OF SUN

Crossing the Ladder of Sun

Poems by

LAURA APOL

Michigan State University Press
East Lansing

∞The paper used in this publication meets the minimum requirements of ANSI/NISO Z39.48–1992 (R 1997) (Permanence of Paper).

Michigan State University Press
East Lansing, Michigan 48823-5245

Printed and bound in the United States of America.

09 08 07 06 05 04 03 1 2 3 4 5 6 7 8 9 10

LIBRARY OF CONGRESS CATALOGING-IN-PUBLICATION DATA
Apol, Laura, 1962–
Crossing the ladder of sun / by Laura Apol.
p. cm.
ISBN 0-87013-685-2 (pbk.: alk. paper)
1. Women—Poetry. 2. Mothers and daughters—Poetry. I. Title.
PS3601.P64C76 2003
811′.6—DC21
2003009748

Cover and interior design by Valerie Brewster, Scribe Typography

Visit Michigan State University Press on the World Wide Web at:

www.msupress.msu.edu

For Jesse and Hanna, my roots and my wings.
And for Stephanie.

Contents

About Wings

Cellular Memory

They say cells remember: each falling star
blazes forever across the dark retina sky.
They say cells remember; mine, stubborn, refuse.

Your hands remind me of someone I loved
but I can't recall who. I think this time I will not forget.
I think it will always be as it is now, forgetting

that once my childless belly was smooth,
once my fingers could recite each scar on each lover's face,
once I believed in God.

Now I wrestle to memory: a bald eagle circling the river,
bats swooping at dusk, one bright-tailed comet
searing a night sky.

I am learning that wings do not always mean flight;
I am learning that sometimes love wakes
where it has fallen asleep.

And so tonight,
when once more my legs twine with yours,
when I feel your breath in my hair as you slip into sleep,

with care I will unlock each living cell.
I will fill it and whisper an urgent *remember,*
remember.

Safe: A Combination

In case of fire, four things matter:
who you are, what you save, where you go,
what you've learned.

Clear four turns left; stop at

forty. Four decades of lilacs when you
wanted roses. You married too young.
Beneath the white veil, your hair shone the color of
flame. *Two turns right until fifty-*

five. Son, daughter, photos, a file, one trip
for yourself. Emerging alone, arms empty with
choice and a hunger within you like
flame. *Back to thirty-*

six. Winter dawn, moments before light and
street silent. Your stride noiseless,
the sun's breath a thin filament of
flame. *Right seventy-*

seven. Primary colors. In case of fire
you know: touch the cardinal and it will sweep
upward. Its wings, bold, are the color of
flame.

From a Traveler Who Does Not Speak French

With prolonged drowning, I have developed gills.
W.H. AUDEN

I have not yet given up breathing,
but I have fallen out of love with words.
Their wild resonance in my chest
sounds more like a heartbeat now,
less like a vowel-and-consonant-shaped voice.

I have fallen in love instead
with the ravenous tones of a saxophone at dusk,
the morning scent of lavender on the stairs,
the almost-still skin of the river, fracturing trees
with its own rippled light.

I have fallen in love with days so clear
you can see Corsica from each hill,
with bougainvillea and laurel blossoms,
smooth Bordeaux, and night swimming as thunder arrives.

In silence, I feel sentences settle
years after they were said;
my skin dampens with Mediterranean mist
even here, miles from the sea.

Now the memory of vespers at Notre Dame
peals, wordless, in my blood.
Chopin, played in St. Julien de Pauvre,
speaks once more in the language of tears.
Rodin's *Kiss* moves from my lips and tongue
into muscle and bone, where it will stay.

Drowning and drowning again,
I inhale mute planets.

I exhale the names of hushed stars.

Ocean

We are the ones who are always hungry,
who stand, mouths open, to catch on our tongues
flakes of impossible ice; who chafe
at the only word we have to describe the kaleidoscope
of crystals: *snow*.

We are the ones with books unread
on the table beside the bed, with music stands ready
and instruments always in tune. We look forever for our names
written faint on the moon.

We are the ones who give life a come-hither look.
We are certain the trees part for us
and the mountains remember.
We plant more than we prune, wake to see islands
rise from the mist.

For us, there is never enough
light. On the edge of the ocean we stand, looking out.
"It is not so big as I had imagined," we sigh.
Its insatiable tongue licks at our feet.

Edge of October (Two Voices)

The cat is herself a text, Shadow
a dark shape curled on your lap, writing
her feline grace into your words;
the low hum in her throat weaves through
each successive draft.

Tell yourself you were stalled in the Horse Latitudes,
not a breath of wind. Only a voice telling you
how happy you are happy you are happy
you are on an ocean smooth as a plate, still
as a cloudless sky, cerulean blue.

Tell yourself you are throwing the
weight overboard to lighten the load:
things you have loved like
poems and letters, music, your children's
dreams. The wind picks up as you go.

Choose a name, not of your father or
lover; a name of resistance, igniting language,
melding the mother tongue. Allow for the fierce taste of
fire, the power of naming: cat, shadow,
bittern, window, lie.

These may be the last fine days of October, its edges
burned brittle—the last ripening of berries,
the last haze of leaves and smoke.
Resettle the cat as you create once more
the woman on the far edge of these words.

Tell yourself she is moving now.
Tell yourself she is saying yes.

Traveling Light

1

Olive drab, he says. Moss green, you think.
It's your traveling dress. Five buttons,
ankle-length skirt, no sleeves.

Like skin, it holds memories of who, of where
you've been. It brushed the grass of an Iowa farm in August,
orchard ripe and pond glinting in the mid-day heat.
It was soaked by Nebraska rain,
dried in Kansas wind and Oklahoma sun.
It walked the edges of rivers without names,
lay on a bed of prairie flowers, counted stars
and city lights from a wall of rocks on a hill.
It saw daybreak in New Mexico,
danced under a Missouri moon,
wandered New Orleans after dark.

Some days it's too cold; some days
it's too hot. Most days it's like breathing—easy.
Just right.

2

You never unpack your bags. Never hang your skirts
in the closet, find a place for your shoes on the floor.
Never did until the day you arrived
and he cleared a corner and invited you in.

Not enough room here for you to stay, he said
as if you might misunderstand and rearrange your life
like the pencils you pushed aside to scatter your earrings
and bracelets on the desk. Not to fear; you had one eye
on the door, kept judging the distance to your waiting car.

But before you showered, before he served pasta
and you brought out Dutch windmill cookies,
he found a hanger and separated shirts
to make a narrow space in his closet.

At first you refused. In the end you hung it after all—
a dress the soft color of moss reaching lower than his shirts,
quietly brushing against them in the dark.

3

You walk through the house a dozen times,
gather up words, music, coffee for the road;
you wear a new T-shirt that tells where you've been.

You think you've said everything you wanted to say,
but walking away, words come at you like driven snow.

You think you've fit yourself into the battered Samsonite
one more time, but hours later you remember
the green dress still there on the closet rod.

Never imagine good-byes can be tidy,
their edges filed off.

In the next town you phone, ask him to mail the dress.

4

Imagine he holds the moss-colored dress in his hands,
buries his face in the folds of the skirt.
Imagine he fingers the buttons—one tidy row of desire.

Once you wore dresses over mandatory slip, hose,
matched bra and panties. Now when you think of this dress
smoothed from your shoulders, you see nothing but skin
polished by light.

5

When the dress arrives, folded in a package
tight with tape, it is still warm. He must have laid it out
on the bed, must have matched the edges of the full skirt,
the shoulders, the seams that run up the back.
The top button is fastened—his work, not yours.

For a moment you forget this is a traveling dress,
forget that your bags lie open, half-packed for another trip.

For a moment you wish you knew how to stay,
wish someone wanted you to,
wish the words folded into the olive-drab dress
sounded less like good-bye.

Magnolias

Yesterday there were magnolias,
cupped like a hand, with petals the silky scent
of a kiss.

Today wind caught those kisses in flight,
turned them like the seasons we've known,
spun them

to the rim of the earth. Fierce heaven
curves toward ocean waves
where angels

repeat your name with the tide.
Somewhere sea and sky
meet

in a moment seamless as spring's flowering.
Perhaps there you will remember
me.

Night Driving

When you drive too late, too long,
whooping cranes rise from the blacktop night,
span the front of the car, rear up sudden
and out of sight. You warn me of this over dinner,
your words a caution I fold into my all-night
cross-country wandering.

Why whooping cranes, I wonder.
Why not common gulls or gold-bellied hawks?
Why not road tar transformed into raven, crow,
shadow-rimmed owl?

Mile after mile, I keep vigil,
search the headlight's glare for those wild white wings,
the long curve of neck, the spindled legs.
I wait their perfect appearance
—the just-right word in a prayer saying *stop here,*
my young son's hand saying *stay,*
insistent love saying *now.*

The twelve-hour road stretches on, each lane
blank as a starless sky. The white dashed lines
never falter, never rise to take flight.

I am near home, eyes gritty, black coffee
cold in a styrofoam cup, when at last cranes appear,
breasts lit with dawn, bright-feathered grace
descending. No whooping cranes, rising;
these wings are your warning
ushering me, safe, into day.

Hanna Teaches Me about Wings

Her slight hand flutters against mine—

my daughter, wide-eyed in the house where
wings (white, pale yellow, black-marked, blue-edged)
pulse and pause and wait,

breathing, breathing against the thick air.

Snow melts on the glass roof as
wings consider our fingers, fanned,
the drift of our shoulders,

slip through her live fire for some safer shade.

At night, her hands work for hours to
touch only the word—red crayon, yellow paper:
BTRFLS.

∞

The winter lover I will not marry knows
my heart has wandered.

I tell him it's about
wings, how I fear having mine pinned. He
disagrees: it's not wings, it's all the other flowers,
he says.

Perhaps he's right. I want them all—purple and blue,
orange, yellow, red passion.

∞

Life cycles: egg to hungry larva
to the knitted pupa's sleep-and-wait.

All week we watch at the threshold of
wings, press faces to the glass box, searching for
shadows unfolding.

One day she hurries to tell me
how they opened, one by one, and fanned air to color;
how the teacher took the box outdoors and
lifted the lid.

Three flew away;

one climbed the teacher's finger, her sleeve,
perched on her shoulder, lit in her white hair—

only then caught the wind and took flight.

∞

A note arrives from a distant friend.

She says the monarchs have come—the skies fill
with them each afternoon, the trees pulse
before dusk.

She wants me to see them; she is sending a gift.

The gift is a box—blue as mid-day, my name
on the lid. Inside, a white cotton square
pillows one perfect monarch, black veined,
an amber mosaic of place.

She found it, already dead, mid-migration.

∞

I wash the skeleton blades of her back,
kneel at the side of the tub
to towel her dry:

head, shoulders, outline of ribs;
little girl hips, thighs, winged shadow
between her thin legs.

She raises her feet—first one, then
the other, steadies herself on my shoulder,
the top of my head. My skin

is alive where she touches, achingly cool
when her fingers let go.

∞

Under the maple—a scatter of hand-shapes
the October color of
wings.

As I watch from the window
a breeze swirls them, wild,
into flight.

River of Then and Now

If you tell me the river is here
I will ask you which river.
Not its name; I ask you
which river?

D. GERBER

You say there is one river, and we crossed it.

I say every river is two: the river it was,
and the river it is becoming. Just as every silence
is the silence it is, and the silence it will be.

We navigate the past on aching wings,

Orion mute in the sky,
winter moon lined with the faces we've known
and will never see again.

Is there one river or two? I only know this:

there is the garden the garden is growing into,
there is the tree the tree is dying toward.

And every long silence has a river in it—
a river that moves on.

The Whole World Between Us

In New York City, 1979

Joe Favata, you were the Italian boy
with the beautiful name I met outside
the cathedral of St. John the Divine on a windy day
half a lifetime ago.

The stories you told were magic
because they were not mine, your Queens
childhood far from my open Iowa fields.

You were the mystery of that whole city in one
afternoon; I fell in love with your world, bright as a
red-checked curtain in a dark paneled room.

I never told anyone whose name was written
on that matchbook cover, the one I carried in my pocket
through more than a decade of flights back,
the one I didn't phone.

March afternoons the wind still carries your voice.

Your amaretto kisses, far from home,
are still the sweetest thing I've known.

Next Time

The children are asleep in the back seat,
their breathing steady and deep as the wing strokes
of the great owl calling to them in their dreams.
Near the rim of the east, the moon is lifting;
driving into it I rise on words we have not spoken—
words carried on the sweet scent of apples,
ripening in the orchard to the hum of bees.

Once again you have taken me in.
And I have drawn sad thank-yous from my bag:
a book I have already wandered; instant coffee the color of dust;
a half-empty jar of sweet peppers.

Next time we will begin mid-sentence,
before you open the door, or I turn off the car.
And I will remember lilacs, dark purple,
and I will not forget to ask the meaning of your name,
as if you were a cave that would spring open.

Such treasures, the stories you hold. In the dark,
driving into the moon, they sing to me without words.

Hanna Teaches Me about Distance

Think of love—how it stretches:
you under hot Texas sun,

me seeing Asia's thick moon and stars,
exactly the whole world between us.

Even the telephone wires crackle;
I hear only half of what you say.

I have never been so far from you, daughter.
The equator pulls taut, a long umbilical;

anywhere I go from here, I am closer to you.

Pilgrimage into Your Past

I know I will make it someday,
whether I tell you or not. What could you say
that would make me change my mind?

I will park on the edge of the town I've never seen
(though in my mind it is always asleep) and walk along Fourth Street
with measured steps. It will be autumn;

the familiar trees will blaze, and I will name each one.
I will find your mother; she will feed me
tart applesauce and pie with perfect peaks of meringue.

Later she'll show me the coal furnace, the hall where you
slept on hot nights, photos I've seen. Right field, home plate,
late-afternoon end zone—I'll learn them with my hands and lungs,

as if learning a place is the same as learning you.
If her eyes are yours and I look into them,
perhaps I will understand more than I do now.

If she sings—even one line—perhaps I will know
the words. And if she pauses to bless me as I go,
perhaps then the road will rise to meet me,

and God at last will hold me in the palm of her hand.

Why I Cannot Tell the Story

The story is too long. Each day it goes out, returns
hungry as geese in a winter field.

You will never understand.

The story is not a map. Polaris steadies the night sky;
no other light guides sailors across the sea.

In the story no one smiles. No lesson is learned.
The narrator cannot change anyone's heart.

The story is a gate to another story,
which opens onto a story after that.

I made it up, but the story is true.

> So ask me instead about the Northern Lights.
> Ask me the names of the islands, the years of the pine
> in the yard.
>
> Ask for a story with heroes—a story that begins
> *Long ago, in a far-away land.*
>
> I will turn my words over like a stone,
> like a shell, like a blossom
>
> held until the red petals fall.

You are far away tonight.
This is not a story that will keep.

The Switch

Someone loves the man who comes to my house
to lay wire. Someone loves the man who pours the concrete,
the one who tears up the shingles, the one who puts in
the studs. Someone loves the man who unrolls
the carpet. I know, because once

I kissed your smooth cheek in the morning
and watched you dress—denim shirt, jeans,
work boots, and a belt heavy with tools.
After you were gone I made coffee, made
the bed, made myself think of something—anything—
besides the heights where you worked, the hot wires
your fingers touched and how I loved those fingers,
the thick palms, the white crescents of your nails.

One day you threw a switch that almost killed you:
sparks, fire, burns that covered your hands and face.
It was before we met, but I saved the story,
took it out in the morning after you'd gone,
recited it like a rosary. I knew I could love you
into safety, pray your world right, smooth your life
like a bead between my fingers.

This morning I say the story again and wonder where you are,
which wires you are touching. Wonder who watches you dress,
who prays over your scars.

And wonder as I pour another cup of coffee just who loves
the man snaking wire from my attic to the basement.
I wonder who is praying for him as, right now,
he is throwing the switch.

Oklahoma Drought

I am hanging laundry under a heavy sky,
hoping the same gods who make every light red when I'm late,
who send the last frost just after my tulips come up,
who lead the neighborhood strays to my trash each Tuesday morning
will not see the parched garden or the yellow-white grass,
but will be tempted instead by this row of towels,
these jeans and white T-shirts, listless in the still air.

We each have our dance to summon rain:
the neighbor washes his car; my best friend schedules a picnic;
my brother leaves the top down on his convertible overnight.

Nothing.

It's not about rain; it's about luck.

I lived on the Mississippi through the flood of '93,
filled sandbags to stop the river rising
over the levee, into the streets, the shops, the homes of people I loved.
I swore then I'd never complain about rain that *wasn't*
—not after days and days of downpours,
storms upstream swelling a river already stretched.

That year people stocked their sudden ponds with catfish, trout,
hoping the fickle deities would see and withhold rain
until there were only circles of mud, fish bones like fine white combs
and a water table low enough to—mercifully—
gather the river back.

Call it tempting fate, playing god;
I will stay here, lightning-rod stiff, looking skyward,

waving a damp white handkerchief.

A Map to the Wilderness

1

The woman toweling her hair
by the side of the pool is not beautiful,
but the light through the windows behind her
makes her seem so: her hands sure as she
pats first her arms, then legs, finally
draping the towel behind her neck.
She leaves soundlessly and the door
swings closed.

This hour, this place
and the rhythm of these strokes—
it is the nearest her world comes to silence.

2

She will taste like fruit:
something wild and dark,
a blackberry, perhaps, filled with seeds.
—not the sweet juice of a peach,
a grape's smooth tranquility,
or the perfect cross-section of an orange.

No, she is blackberry tang, blackberry bramble;
hers are the thorns that draw blood.

3

She cannot decide whether she is running
to or *from*. Or what. She knows
it's not the hills that slow her, it's the wind—
wind that pushes words and breath inside,
makes *exhale* the same as *inhale*,
takes away choice.

Each hill, she knows,
has a down side, but wind—wind can change
around each corner.

4

The woman at rest in the sun
looks sadder than her years,
as if she cannot stop arguing with herself,
even for the sake of a dream.
She wishes she could make it easy,
find answers that are not circles,

untangle mysteries that raise their heads, dark,
even as she sleeps in light.

5

She has moved the ironing to the doorway,
lets the shirt sleeves hang out the open sliding glass,
moves surely across collars, shoulders,
and pockets. This is no caress; there is no
motion lost. She irons blouses to Pachelbel,
presses pleats to Vivaldi, smoothes seams to Corelli.
She chooses baroque because they thought the world
made sense.

She chooses the doorway
because it lets her pretend the world outside
includes her.

6

She wished for a map. Which is not, after all,
what she needs. No secret: water and thorns,
wind, sun, and duty.

Mostly she wants to be more
than the words that define her.

Not Only on the Island

You say it is all a poem:

orchard, rising moon, vivid canopy of leaves.
White lip of the autumn sea.

Perhaps you are right: waterlilies bloom
beneath the artist's brush, a kiss is born
from the sculptor's clay.

We write the poems
we think we may have lived.

The ring my lover threw to the waves
will never wash ashore, but here it is,
unkept promise at the center of my words,

proving nothing is ever lost.

So I hang laundry
as if September sun were all that mattered,
as if indigo, salmon, moss-green shirts on a line
were a story of their own.

I gather the last pears from the backyard tree,
slice ivory crescents into a bowl.

Tonight I will write you a letter.
I will tell you what I can no longer find.
I will add sand and broken shells from a day we shared.

You will open it and remember the lone seal
that followed the tide. You will remember rocks
and a gray sky.

You will remember everything we thought
but never said, everything we said
but then forgot.

You will already be writing a poem.

Mid-Flight

Nothing Begins with Us

—not this story nor any other.

Andromeda does not slow her dizzying spin
nor does a field of wheat
wait. We catch our plane

in flight; below us, time
fades like a prim border of pines
while the sky opens wide as
god's blue eye.

We have far to go, navigating
between stars that appear only
after dark. The secret names

we were given at birth are cradled
in our curved hands.

It is a magic

world now, and we are at
the center, our own lives the map,

our words the edge of a knife
we are just beginning to hone.

Hanna Teaches Me about Writing

BIRTH

I was wonce waking alog a path made of sillk. I did not see the spidere that I was coming owt of, that terwerld me arowd and rapped me up. She fot wen thay teride to wash me and finally got me bake. When I looked up at her agen… I saw a wonderfol thing… a mother smiling done at me as if to say I like you. I felt at home safe in my mothers haert and ames and I felt welcemd in to the wrold.

HANNA, AGE 8

She catches words mid-flight,
writing her birth
as if she had been there—

cocoon she broke out of,
silk thread she slid on,
push and tug
of a waiting mother's heart.

What does she know—

daughter born hand first,
lunging into light,
wanting her own world more than
she wanted me

—what does she know of that first
wordless cry?

It is her story now, line after line.

I am actor in her play,
woman assigned a part,
nothing to say—

my body the passage into her life,

my silence her blank page.

Two A.M.

Strange to me: motherhood,
this way of women,
my way now.

Dreams no longer whole,
shaped by stirrings in the night,
interrupted by the rush of milk.

Even as the baby sleeps, I wake,
tense, waiting for the cry
as did my mother, and her mother.

Those still moments:
thoughts, a small bird, trapped in flight;
bent wings throb against smooth glass,

stain bright blood.
In the dark-caught breath of silence,
startling—a cry.

Stretch Marks

You wear their names on your body—
across breasts, curve of hips, once-smooth
span of belly,

your children's names imprinted on your skin.
Some women (whose selves live contentedly
in the bodies of others) call this

a source of pride, a badge of motherhood
which makes you, female, at last complete,
a hero of sorts. You see it

as the aching story engraved in flesh
of how you've changed, a sign to be read
like tree rings or strata of rocks,

line after widening line.

Woman of Light

for Lucille Clifton

Lucille, whose name means light
and whose dark eyes are light as well,
Lucille, I am the woman in the second row,

white, with skinny hips and a colorless blouse,
loving the turquoise you shimmer—the bright,
the long and the curve of it,

your words in my hands, your voice in my ears;

Tell me again, Lucille, about the poems
you lost and the babies you saved.

Tell me you couldn't replace
the children, tell me you could
replace the poems; please, tell me that lie
again because I, too, have poems and children

and some days they play side by side,
tossing sound back and forth;

some days they fight to the death.

You say your children won, but we both know
that lost poems are poems lost forever;
like lightning, words won't strike the same place
again.

Tell me that truth, strong woman of light;
please, tell me that hard truth.

Father Reading

Before bed my father read to me
—poems that rhymed, their riderless
ta-dum ta-da-dum ta-da-dum galloping
like the Highwayman's horse by moonlight.
I dreamed red ribbons woven in raven hair,
a man at the window with lace at his throat,
and love.

It was a life I expected:
the romance of the inevitable,
the future a rhyme I could always predict.

So I went to a college he knew,
married a man he approved,
had two blonde children (a boy and a girl).
I cleaned on Fridays, baked on Saturdays,
picked up toys and dirty clothes
at bedtime as I'd been taught:
ta-dum ta-da-dum ta-da-dum.

And I wrote what we knew I would:
clean lines, their tidy syllables
prancing past discontent,
the sharp stones of regret, the sheer drop
of anger unanswered.

When truth mattered more than meter
I saw clenched fists around me that
were not mine.

Then they were.

And I heard a different story:
the landlord's daughter pulls the trigger,

shatters her own breast.
I packed my bags, gathered my words,
let the highwayman ride to his death—
ta-da-dum —no woman as warning
slumped over the musket's muzzle.

And I wondered:
how could a father embrace a daughter
with lines fixed as poetic foot and meter?
How could he weave love
with blood-red ribbons and lace?

And what of closure, the door
ending the poem with a click—

no click of hot flint striking powder,
but the click of a lock catching
as a woman walks away.

Meteors, Late Summer, 1993

More than a lifetime it takes
when a star goes dead
for the darkness to arrive.
J. HOLDEN

But arrive it does, sudden dark rewriting the sky
as we've known it — falsely — for years.

No one notes the fireflies shifting
from lion to winged horse to queen's chair,
drifting to dark. Lightning strikes an oak
and the tree stands, only the bark exploding
in a rift of new wood the length of the trunk.
Thunder echoes forever through that fissure

— there are things we never escape.
Our lives stretch behind us, trailing fire.
Summer nights, my husband's dreams hinged
to the hum of a box fan while I danced with the hunter,
lost myself in the light of his studded belt,
his raised club, the bloody gash in his shoulder.

Once, Betelgeuse was our word for love
when together we plotted the curve of
its red light. Magnitude is relative,
and cycles and circles appear if you wait.
Who can wait long enough?

When Betelgeuse fades from the sky, who will know?
When its darkness arrives,
will Orion — a slow lifetime later — be whole?

Ending a Marriage: Six Lessons

1: THE WEDDING RING

She said it snags her glove
when he asked. Truth is, it snags much more—
catches on conversation, unraveling years of words.

Those are sharp gold prongs,
pressing a name strange as ice
to her tongue.

So he claims she is cold—
a woman of metal and hard stone, forgets
the days of heat pulsing through her fingers,

never sees the woman who wants only
to slide her hand, smoothly,
into her own skin.

2: LEARNING TO BREATHE

His hands around my throat carve the word *love love*
love in my skin

and the air is as thin as in the mountains I never learned
not to climb.

I am showing him edges at every turn—
loose stones slipping under our feet and trees jutting from rock.

He sees only a four-lane road, smooth,
that stretches forever.

He will build it, he says, carve up this wild place.
He believes in miracles worked by his own two hands.

I see a narrow trail, overgrown with brush and scrub
skirting precipice and walls of earth.

It is wide enough for one.
There is space there to walk, and air—

air enough to breathe.

3: MENDING

The day we parted, when the future was simply
a gash in our lives and the past was a series
of frayed edges,

that day we did not kiss one last time.
We did not wash the sheets,
mop the floors, take out the trash.

You sat at the machine,
I picked up a needle and thread and,
across the table where we'd shared

so many meals, we stitched—
as always, your stitches tight, even, sure,
mine loose and haphazard.

Still, there is something to be said for mending
on such a day:

there is the wisdom of knowing which things
can be salvaged;

there is the art of choosing the right stitch.

4: A LETTER TO HIS SISTER

Last night I dreamed you had forgiven me
—not the around-the-table kind of forgiveness,
but the open-the-door-a-crack kind.

And you let me in.

I told you the truth. Not the whole truth
—no bruises or holes punched in walls.
Just what I could tell: we stopped talking, grew apart,
had no choice. Too late, too late, I chanted to your
smooth-bead remedies; still you went on.

Before leaving, I took a picture of everyone who had once been
my family, and though they did not smile, they did not turn.
We were all polite.

It was an early morning dream,
the kind that does not leave with dawn. The kind that
waits inside the cup of coffee, the sting of the shower's spray,
the stranger on the bus.

You will never read this letter, though all day
I imagined you had, imagined you could hear the whole truth
and I could say it—out loud—so your parents would understand.

Say it so your sons would once more speak to me.
Loud so your daughters would one day learn my name.

5: AN ANNIVERSARY POEM FOR MY EX-HUSBAND

It is not a door I open often: once a year, the second
night of June. There is a woman, dressing slowly—
white gown, garter and veil. She will not let you watch.

You will sing her down the aisle
because you know the words. You were good
for leaning on, I remember that. You could fix the world

like you fixed the vacuum, the heater core,
the squeaky headboard on the bed.

One day you built a shelf for my clock
as a newlywed surprise and I thanked you
the whole afternoon. I should have thanked you
longer

and you should have loved me more. Last week
in the back of a drawer, our son found your ring.
He's been wearing it for days
and I see fingers

I thought I had forgotten. There is no
forgetting: the woman is still there, the second night
of June, adjusting her veil, walking slowly
into your song. And once more you hold out

your familiar hand.

6: CLEAVING

The night before my ex-husband remarried,
I wasn't there to see the lightning. I was states away,
holding my world together with a friend and a bottle
of cabernet. (The night before my own wedding—*leave father*
and mother, cleave to each other, one flesh—I was too young
to buy a bottle of wine or even order a drink.)

I learned about the lightning later,
when the neighbor met me on the driveway,
told me that Friday night there had been
a storm, and look (she pointed to bark in the grass at our feet,
led me behind the house
to the pine at the center of my yard)
look where the lightning struck;

look how the bark blew off in a spiral the length of the trunk
(we were walking around the 70-foot tree—around and around),
look how the new wood exploded from the heart,
how the split circled from the tip to the base; and look here
(yards from the trunk), how the roots leapt from the ground
with the force of the charge.

From a distance, the tree seems exactly the same
—still standing, still green. I had thought lightning would cleave
a tree in two, a clean split. (Later I learned
lightning doesn't split—it heats the water in the tree,
which explodes, finding its own way out.)

The neighbor went home. I wandered the grass, slowly,
gathering pieces of bark, long splinters of pine.

Then I poured a glass of cabernet and drank it outside,
in the back yard. Alone.

The Grass Is on Fire

Waiting for Grief

You say grief is an old friend, but each day
her dark head

bobs silent past your window at dawn.
She has chased the birds from your trees,
and whispers through the empty pods of the mimosa
a language forgotten at birth.

Alone at night, you candle your injured heart;
light shines through the shell but at the center
you see no bruise.

Grief has broken every vow she made—
found some new love, turned her eyes
from your open hands. You burn
for the taste of her.

Just when you think she will not return,
you find her asleep in your bed. Her hair is undone
and she stirs in her dreams.

If you are tempted to rouse her,
remember—on the rim of her sleep
your pain is engraved.

She wakes soon enough.

Synchronicity

We got the call

the morning I found
feathers
at the door.

The gray cat's
summer jay?
I saw

one blue wing fall
through autumn
constellations

seventh sister
setting
sail

my grandmother
alone
that night

slipping her skin.

Miscarriage

It is as if the tree caught fire,
and with it we who are words, spoken,
never speaking. *David:* time's deeply drawn
breath burst dark in the womb.

Long have I prayed
for one aching moment of you warm,
shaped to the curve of my breast.

Silent tongues, dry tinder, flame
and flame again. Yours is the name
I cradle in my sleep.

A Talk about Trees

> *What kind of times are they, when*
> *a talk about trees is almost a crime*
> *because it implies silence about so many horrors?*
> B. BRECHT

All week the new-pruned trees have oozed
their watery sap. Tears river the bark,
spatter the ground beneath, staining the patio,
the driveway, gumming the car doors.

By day, I grieve the lost limbs,
phantoms haunting a dream once green.
By night, the moon waxes full,
hanging in the shorn maple, the empty elm,
stark in the window now, bleak over the bed.

The late-night radio reports the next ways of war.
On my ceiling, unfamiliar lights shine
from the neighbor's yard.

Distance has ceased to exist.

Before dawn, my daughter wakes me with her cries.
Bad dream, bad dream she calls through the house,
rushing to curl beneath my covers and sob her terror:
men with masks coming for us, Mom;
we grabbed buckets of tar to seal ourselves in the car.

She curves her girlbody to the question mark
I have become. I circle her with my arm.
We pretend I can keep her safe.

At the window, the blinding moon waits.

Scars

He told me the story before we married, before
I met his family or walked the farm where he'd
grown up: how as a child he'd played alone,
catching footballs he kicked high enough to run under;
lobbing baseballs onto the shed, then fielding pop flies;

building ramps for his red sting-ray bike—
ramps that sent him, arm first, through the window
of the garage.

Blood beat from the gash in a pulsing arc,
but when he opened the back door
his mother swept him out,
left him standing, red stain soaking the grass
while she fetched a rag and plastic for the car and the long drive
to town, to the doctor and 45 stitches that crawled across
his inner arm.

For twelve years my tongue traced
that shiny snag, caught on the bright hook
in his flesh, repeating the story as if it were mine.
The thirteenth year, I stopped.

I could have sworn I'd thrown that memory back,
but today someone says *scar* and I taste it,
touch for an instant that tender place,
and see again a young boy
bleeding cleanly into the grass.

Anorexia

Having lived her life
in a body intent on consuming
itself,

she welcomes this soft-rounding belly,
the curve of hips,
the thickening of thighs.

For her mother, she was always good—
blouse tucked tight into
sharp pleated slacks;

for her father, she was perfect—
smiling daughter
in a size-three bikini.

For herself she was hungry—
silent inside her own bones,

nothing more to devour,
brittle elbows and wrists

her only voice.

Learning to Dance

It wasn't the dancing my parents feared as much as
the *where*—dens of wine, sin and song,
though the only bar in town, Docs,
never had so much as a radio, and the regulars there
could no more dance than fly.

Still, I imagined dance floors and discos
with doors like black holes
that would suck me from the sidewalk,
far down the street, that would never let me
go. I stayed away.

My first dance lesson: fifteen, and a boy I knew
taught me a few steps at his house. His parents came home
too soon; the lesson was short but good.

My first real dance: after hours at the roller rink
outside town. I went with the preacher's kid who'd stashed
a six-pack in his car; he held me so close our bodies
threw sparks. Then he puked on my shoes and his father
drove us home.

My first dance floor: New York City on a school trip.
A thirst for adventure led to a bar off Times Square
where a man the age of my father asked me
to dance. His hands were faster than his feet;
he offered me money in a language
I did not understand.

And so I have learned the *where*
without learning to dance. And tonight I walk into Ford's Place
where the band is loud enough and the drinks stiff enough
to make you forget things you don't know.

I sit alone at a table near the front.
I've been seeing the lead guitarist because I like how
he plays the blues. But tonight it's all rock
and the dance floor is crowded with faces that shift, surface,
re-couple after each song and another shot.

Men wear boots and brass buckles, phallic keys
hanging from pockets and belt loops. They strut, use *fuck*
as a noun. The women are adjectives: tight pants, cheap dye,
lipstick so red it hurts.

And me. I feel colorless, clean,
exuding light that tugs at the hawking men at the bar. Drink?
Thanks; got one. Darts? *Rather hear the band.* Dance?
Never learned.

Never learned. What's to learn but what I already know:

We are lonely people wishing to touch. The woman whose
nipples show through her blouse; the man whose wife is a *bitch*
and whose girlfriend, a *whore*; the band breathing smoke,
giving all of us something to dance to.

It's all here: my first love, my first dance, my first bar.
I believe I am Other and refuse what they offer.
But I too am tipping my beer, tapping my foot,
waiting for last call

and wishing for someone to drive me home, safely,
through dark.

Canon

The woman is trying to tell me something the woman crying
in the middle of the dark street wandering from her own parked
car to mine the woman with the black terrier cradled in her arms

she is trying to tell me the dog is dying the black dog hit by
some other car that didn't stay she is trying to tell me
the dog in her arms is dying

But my radio is playing Pachelbel—
evening music. Once you said the Canon in D

was your favorite (it is mine, too),
your passion born from one night

with a cellist who had passion of her own.
Though she left, that music never stopped.

Now because we love the same canon
my thoughts turn back, follow you home like

the black terrier cradled in the woman's arms the woman
crying in the dark street crying for a stray dog hit by a car that
didn't even stop the woman walking toward my car

the woman who is weeping for a stray black dog
trying to tell me something the woman trying to tell me
the dog in her arms is dead.

Chicago

Full moon tonight, rising through the windows
over my bed. I try not to close my eyes,
afraid that if I do, *la luna* will worry and worry
the edges of my dreams.

Last time I saw a moon like this
was from the Ferris wheel on Navy Pier.
I was afraid of heights. I was afraid of water.
I was afraid of the dark, but more afraid
of your hand on my shoulder:

you were what I thought I loved.

Darling, I tried to sleep with my eyes open
in all those ruined cities: San Francisco,
Montreal, Boston, Baton Rouge.
Sometimes while I dozed
you stripped the rings from my fingers,
stole the hoops from my ears.

That night in Chicago,
while you thought I was asleep
you traced the curve of my thigh,
breathed into my hair.

But I caught your true face by the city lights.

Tonight, lying in moonlight,
there is no face to see; you were everything
you promised not to be.

I was right to be afraid, darling. I was right
not to fall asleep.

Hanna Teaches Me about Daddy-Long-Legs

She reminds me in the camp washroom
— gangly spiders on every sink —

that daddy-long-legs taste like peppermint.
It's a comfort she's saved from last year
when she was afraid and someone offered the promise
of mint-flavored legs.

I wait for her to ask about mommy-long-legs,
but she's too old, just returned
from summer with her father, a tall man
who keeps a spotless house.

So today she remembers the safety of peppermint

— and I remember my own father,
the chalky mints he pressed to my palm
during Sunday sermons, his long legs
crossed in the comfortless wood pews,
words falling like brimstone around me

> *God the Father shouting I was not*
> *a perfect God the Father shouting I was*
> *not God the Father shouting*

— and I remember the fragments of last night's dream,
the steep hill and an infant rolling away,
beyond my reach, faster than I can run.

The grass is on fire behind us.
There is no safety, I think.

Twin Sister, Stillborn

> *liana* — (Fr. to bind): Any luxuriantly growing vine that roots in the ground and climbs, as around a tree trunk.

I am the one who knew you,
the only one who will ever know.

I felt the push of your new heart,
the swim of your limbs, the turn of your self
as you turned toward me. We were wild fish,
smooth wet dancers side by side,
entwined. Our cells divided

then our selves divided and
in a liquid mirror we were a double face
with identical sightless eyes,
same nubby fingers, same zippered spines.

If they had known we were us,
had seen through the stretched wall into
the cave of our shared life,

they would have seen two shadows
bobbing and would have sung lullabies
twice. They would have found
a name that could divide

not into half, but evenly into itself.

And then they would have seen
one shadow quiet,
one wild fish fail, forever imprinting loss
in the growing bones of the other.

By the time I rushed us into the world,
one name was all we needed—
a name for me.

Forty years later,
I choose our birth–death–day
to name you now.

Lianna, tenacious vine holding me,

I have called your unnamed name
across the years, never knowing you
were the absence I was trying to fill, the end
of a sentence I didn't know how to begin.

I am echo to your silence,

you are the loss I took all these years
to find.

Crossing the Ladder of Sun

One Night

You go to bed like any other night,

recounting the day under smooth sheets
and a goose-down quilt, the dog in the kitchen
thumping her tail at the scent of her
marvelous dreams.

The next morning it's different:

an aneurysm explodes, a bomb rips through
concrete, the backache is cancer, the teenage daughter
never comes home.

The miracles of an early spring
cannot make up for this. The unfolding of lilacs
will never steady the world.

Years from now you will tell the story of
a day in March when you paused to feed the dog,
which put someone else at the corner when the car
barreled through, left someone else dead
by the side of the road.

You will say it, but it does not prove the existence of God.

Think of the dog—
how she sleeps with her eyes half-open.
Her nose twitches, her ears perk long before sound at the door.
She knows it's a dangerous world. Still she follows faithfully
the trail of her dreams.

At night your hand on her resting head is god
enough. Your breath in the dark room
is all she needs of grace.

Umbilical

for William Stafford

Eight dollars was too much for
a book of poems — yours or any other —
in graduate school, a baby on the way.
Lifelines are seldom free.

In the end I used the week's
bus fare, remembering
my grandfather stringing ropes
in Midwest blizzards —

intricate webs, house
to barn to shed and
back — like stars to a sailor, a child's
trail of white pebbles in moonlight.

And all week I walked, even the day you
came to class and read aloud lines
I'd marked: lines about maps,
bells, the whine that links

puppy to wolf — *a banner of woe,* you
called that cry. It was a winter
Wednesday, rain
freezing like glass, smooth as

the pen you used to
sign my book. Edging home
that night, I was shell brittle,
glazed with ice;

but your words were the cord that
pulled me, howling, through the storm,
and, wet and slippery,
delivered me.

Remembering Eden

I remember Eden, though I have forgotten
everything else I lost in this life or the others:
the cello line of the Trout Quintet,
the ocean-wide circles of gull, the silvery silk
of my newborn son's hair.

I have forgotten the name of the first boy
I kissed by moonlight under a maple.
I no longer recall the feel of the stillborn sister
who grew beside me in the womb, the lavender scent
of my grandmother's pillow, the morning sounds
of doves under the eave.

But I remember Eden. As if every tree were *that* tree—
knowledge shimmering like light in its leaves.
As if every voice were god's: whale song, hum of locust,
wild coyote howl.

As if everyone I've loved guarded their soul
with a fiery sword, and the way to the land we've lost
had grown over with vines, left only to memory
and dreams.

Blueberries

All right, I will say it then:
I would not have fallen in love again
if it had not been for the blueberries—
acres of them, ripe for picking.
And the gulls. And the miles of sand.
I could have grown old alone.

I would not have fallen in love again
if the cabin had not been red,
aflame in the trees, far back from the road.
Looking from the window at night
there was no sea, no sand, no sky—
only the soft sound of stars circling.

And I would not have fallen in love again
if the waves did not follow each other forever,
if the tide did not reshape the shore
with each visit. Year by year the sea
pulls closer, reclaiming that stretch of sand
we call ours.

Seagulls, the beach, a place to grow old:
Sometimes love bursts sweet on the tongue
—the indigo taste of fresh berries.

Late Winter

She loves him each day for scattering seed on snow.
He sees no connection between passion and feeding birds.

This is a long season — the longest they've known.
Back home where they fell in love, spring is already pushing
through brown grass, exploding along tense branches.
Tuned to that rhythm, his blood says they have survived.

But his still-white breath whispers against the bones of trees.

At night they rub skin on skin to stay warm.
His hand cradles her breast; she sleeps in the curve of his arm.
When gray sun seeps dimly through their east,
he rises to pour coffee.

Then he feeds the birds.

Millet over the crust of snow. Sunflower hearts on the drive.
Thistle seed on the walk near the pine.
By the time she wakes, there are cardinals
(nearly a dozen), jays, chickadees, dark-eyed juncos.

He knows he will tug them daily into spring.

She knows birds fly where they will. But still

they know the hand that cups the seed, the arm that
each morning sweeps a wide arc of blessing.
They rise at the sight of him — far into winter,
long before green.

Pedernal

It belongs to me; God told me if I painted it enough,
I could have it.

G. O'KEEFFE

So you knew if you kept painting it,
the Pedernal would be yours.

But how much was enough, Georgia?
And what does it mean for God to give someone
a mountain?

∞

If painting
and painting again
gave you that mountain,

then perhaps I have written my way

to the baby asleep at night,
cardinals in the evergreen,
love—

(near things—brush
in the valley beneath
the mountain, not the mountain
itself).

∞

You painted flowers, opening,
exposing through color
their bright centers. Did God give you
irises, lilies, red
poppies?

You painted bones. Did God give you
skeletons, the skulls of sheep
under the desert sky?

∞

So Georgia,

when at last I have learned
how much is enough,
then I will name those things
I want like your mountain:

my stillborn twin sister,
sensation in my mother's hands,
Kathy's breasts back without cancer,
and more.

I will write my list
until God grants it: a list insistent

as the desert light, stubborn
as the memory of chase and sleep, determined

as the rock face of Pedernal
and a woman's hand, over and over
drawing the mountain
near.

Learning What Is Enough

1

This time of year, it's the hawks I love, fringed wings,
pale bellies, hooked beaks. I love them in trees,
at rest on posts, rising from near-empty fields.

Mostly I love them in flight.
They know what they know about riding those currents,
resting on air.

2

The sky fades from pink to rose to dark.
I wonder if you know how lovely you are,
your hair falling forward, the crystal of your goblet
catching the last sun.

I would paint this moment like a vivid
crescent of moon, like the pond's edge furred
with snow, weave it through the twilight sounds
of BeauSoleil's *Chanson,* wood crackling in the stove.

3

Our good-byes happen so loudly now, and so often.

Nearby, each weed, each blade of grass,
each pine needle is outlined by crystals of snow;
beyond, the world disappears, clouds rub the corners off
sight, and the world is all gentle.

The ringed disk of sun appears, vanishes,
time after time.

4

In a perfect world, my hands would know *Für Elise*
as yours do, never faltering.

As it is, I am more blessed with zeal than with skill.
But when I stroke those keys, I do it with passion.

I do it with passion, and it is enough.

The Way We Fit Ourselves to It

I am stopping here to try a new posture,
to try to determine if it is the place
or the way we fit ourselves to it that counts.
M. HOGAN

Here there are only faint tracks in red dirt,
a deer trail that follows its thirst
through late-winter grass.
Here the tiny orange flowerings in the season's stubble
are named; so is the crested bird on the fence,
the dust that flames the night sky.

But my friend, we are more than our names.
When I wrap you in hours of talk, I forget to tell you
I have noticed the ring you no longer wear;
I forget to mention there are longer silences between your laughs.
I neglect to thank you for your step next to mine
long after stars come out.

These days I'm thinking of snow—
not the sodden one-day wetness of this place
but the white on white world-snow of my childhood:
drifts and banks, thinly crusted, powder beneath.
I'm thinking of the black gloves I wore one year
and the way flakes settled on my dark palms.
If I had stayed there, hands upturned,
they would have covered me—ice maiden,
woman of snow.

Instead I chose red-dirt warmth,
spread breadcrumbs like a promise,
watched the cardinal with her bright beak winter in my yard,
drawn by my wish and a row of red holly.

If I have fallen into this place
—like dusk, or berries from a backyard bush—
then *place* is not so far from *love* as I may have thought.

So for now let me say I would rather be here;
I would rather be here than anywhere.

see me beautiful

see me beautiful by firelight candlelight
starshine the Pleiades on my back
in grass in leaves beneath you beautiful

with children with women meteor showers
swinging through night dancing smooth
feet slide me beautiful

over wine over coffee black eyes glowing
forward into story song lakeside path to
day to moon rising wild coyote see me

beautiful asleep away running
wind with words with apple tongue with almond
kisses kite string beautiful see how

you make me shine

Happiest Day

1

Write and tell them how happy you are
my husband used to say when he was my husband
and I was not happy.

Chasing monarchs in a field of purple clover
with my son—then I was happy.

Walking with my daughter in the woods
singing *Where have all the flowers gone?*
or *We shall overcome*—I was happy then, too.

The day you took me
to dip my feet in the Mississippi,
the day you took me there, I told you then
I was happy.

And I was.

2

Pastan's poem is called "The Happiest Day"
and I bristle.

Who can say *happiest* I wonder—
choose one day, a single configuration of loves,
a solitary current in the stream?

Think how the present re-visions the past:
how *now* bleeds color into *then.*

A child grown makes the kite more red,
the sky more blue;

my mother's MS
makes that day at the ocean more sweet.

Each loss makes dearer the ordinary *before*:
before the fire, the flood,
the broken vase, the wilted flowers.
Before anyone answered the phone.

3

Best. Greatest. Most wonderful.
You speak in superlatives, and I hear
comparison, implied competition.

You say it's not comparing—only gratitude so sweeping
language fails to follow,

a threshold of grace crossed and re-crossed
with each closing day.

4

I still don't know how to read a river.
And here, by a bend in a river called Grand,
I wonder if, perhaps, this is *happiest.*

I've made a life's work of wishing: first stars,
coins in fountains, meteorites searing the sky.

Now, my only wish is what I have this day:

translucent leaves unfurling outside my high window,
daughter's cartwheels in the grass,
son fingering a nocturne that moves me time and again;

finch's song, morning coffee, afternoon skin on skin;

your eyes, with the coming of dark, saying
best.

Hanna Teaches Me about Monkey Bars

When is she ever more beautiful than this:

shining, as hand over hungry hand
she crosses the ladder of sun
swinging herself forward
into day, willowy arms strong,
shoulders taut,

so in love with her own body
I can hardly bear it.

Now she grasps every bar, now every other,
her reach lengthening,
forward, back.

I have drifted naked in a bayou,
run marathons mile after mile,
burrowed toes into fine white sand,

but I have never loved my body like this.

She glides easy through this dance,
drops to the sawdust
and climbs to cross again, again, again.

My eyes follow as, clear-winged, she rises
and soars.

Acknowledgments

My sincere gratitude to the writing groups and writers who across time have provided encouragement and feedback on these poems in various forms: from the Oklahoma years—Valerie Saad, Carol Koss, Jane Taylor, Judith O'Brien, Joan Moore, Carl Sennhenn, Tina Kambour, Sarah Webb, Richard Dixon; from the Michigan years—Jay Featherstone, Leonora Smith, Dick Thomas, Laurence Maxwell; and from the Florida summers—Charley Rutherford, Dean Flower, Ginny Armstrong, Rich Drozd, and Al and Priscilla Clemente.

Thanks, too, to the friends who have tolerated—and even invited—having poems thrust upon them: Carol Mason-Straughan, Stephanie Jordan, Twila Konynenbelt, Jane Farrell, Carl Vandermeulen, Tony Clay, Nancy Huse, Christine Root, Rachelle Apol, Kathy and T.H. Milby, Mark Becker, Rand Spiro, and Ralph Tucker.

Finally, my most heartfelt thanks to the people whose suggestions for revisions are found so often in these poems, and in my life: Stephanie Alnot, David Pimm, and Anita Skeen. To each, as writers and friends, I owe an enormous debt.

I would also like to acknowledge my appreciation to the Michigan State University Office of the Vice President for Research and Grants for support in completing this manuscript; to my department chair, Stephen Koziol, for helping create time and recognition for poetry in my professional life; and to Martha Bates, a dedicated editor—and now friend—at the MSU Press.

Some of the poems in this volume were originally published in the following journals and anthologies:

"Umbilical," *The Hudson Review;* "Father Reading," *Red Cedar Review;* "Safe: A Combination," *Object Lesson;* "Night Driving," *Bluestone Review;* "Next Time" and "Learning What Is Enough," *Sistersong: Women Across Cultures;* "Two A.M.," *Blue Unicorn;* "Blueberries," *Whole Notes;* "In New York City, 1979," *Lyrical Iowa;* "Woman of Light" and "Miscarriage," *Claiming the Spirit Within* (Boston, Mass.: Beacon Press, 1997); "Stretch Marks," *I Am Becoming the Woman I've Wanted* (Watsonville, Calif.: Papier Maché Press, 1994); "Hanna on the Monkey Bars," *Living Out Loud* (Oklahoma City, Okla.: Individual Artists of Oklahoma, 1999); "Nothing Begins with Us" (as "First Night of Class"), *In Praise of Pedagogy* (Portland, Maine: Calendar Islands Publishers, 2000).